HOW CAN TWO WALK TOGETHER

Daniel Nana Kwame Opare

How Can Two Walk Together
Copyright © 2015 by **Daniel Nana Kwame Opare**. All rights reserved.

No part of this publication may be reproduced, stored in a retrieval system or transmitted in any way by any means, electronic, mechanical, photocopy, recording or otherwise, without the prior permission of the author except as provided by USA copyright law.

All characters appearing in this work are fictitious. Any resemblance to real persons, living or dead, is purely coincidental.

The opinions expressed by the author are not necessarily those of Revival Waves of Glory Books & Publishing.

Published by Revival Waves of Glory Books & Publishing
PO Box 596| Litchfield, Illinois 62056 USA
www.revivalwavesofgloryministries.com

Revival Waves of Glory Books & Publishing is committed to excellence in the publishing industry.

Book design copyright © 2015 by Revival Waves of Glory Books & Publishing. All rights reserved.

EBook: 978-1-329-10798-4
Paperback: 978-1-329-10795-3
Hardcover: 978-1-329-10797-7

Published in the United States of America

TABLE OF CONTENTS

PREFACE 5
Author... 6
Acknowledgment... 7
Dedication 8
CHAPTER ONE **Types of Human Nature** 9
    CHOLERIC... 10
    SANQUINE 16
    MELANCHOLY 24
    PLEGMATIC 33
    SUPINE 38
    BESIDE THE TEMPERATMENTS 46
    MESSAGE TO MEN CONCERNING WOMEN.............. 47
CHAPTER TWO **Peace Medicine** 50
    OFFENCE 50
    ANGER 52
    APOLOGY 56
    FORGIVING 58
    LOVE 60
About the Author 63

PREFACE

It is written. "Behold, how good and how pleasant it is for brethren to dwell together in unity". (Psalm 133)

Where there is unity there is peace and development. But unity cannot be achieved unless people know themselves by nature.

For this reason, this book has been written to make people aware, of the different kinds of human nature in order to make right choices for marriage, friendship and leadership, as well as career, profession and occupation.

This book will also enable people to know the peace, medicine in order for peace which serves as the sources of unity and development in life, society and a nation as a whole, to prevail.

The Bible says, that, "My people are destroyed for lack of knowledge".

This book is full of divine truth. Read it to be wiser.

All the quotations in this book were taken from the Gideon International Version of the Bible

AUTHOR

Daniel N. K. Opare

E-mail:roselmaclean@yahoo.com

nagasnagasty@aol.com

Tel.: +233(0)20 / + (0)26 9851768

Acknowledgment

I thank God, the owner of the universe for bestowing upon me wisdom and insight to write this book.

I also thank my parents–Kweku Larbi, Leticia Agyeibea, Johnson N. K. Budu and pastor D. K Awhireng whose contributions have brought me this far.

DEDICATION

To: My loved ones.

CHAPTER ONE

Types of Human Nature

The Bible says in amos3: 3 that, "How can two walk together unless they agree"? The question is, how can they agree? They can agree when they understand themselves. And how can they understand themselves? They can understand themselves by knowing themselves by nature.

Human nature is defined as the basic character of a person.

Problems, including sickness can only be solved or prevented when the sources is discovered; hence, discovery leads to problem solving.

Lack of knowledge of human nature normally generates problem between leaders and subordinates, couples, friends and relatives.

Many people make wrong choices in choosing life partners, leaders, career, profession or occupations due to lack of knowledge of human nature. Knowledge of human nature reduces offense as well as anger.

People may look alike in identity, but completely different in character. Identical twins are always different in character.

However, everyone is so special and unique with special character traits, yet there are several common character traits known as temperaments among mankind. Out of these numerous common character traits among human beings, there are five commonest known as basic temperaments. These are choleric, sanguine, melancholy, phlegmatic and supine.

CHOLERIC

Undoubtedly, choleric are born leaders. They form the highest percentage of powerful and fearless leaders in the world, nations, societies; institutions and organizations. They possess great leadership qualities and abilities. They are capable of leading and inspiring small, medium, and large number of people for great achievements.

Choleric is fast-paced personalities. Hence, they always demand that things be done correctly and swiftly. They prefer working at a very fast paced; in a military fashion. Do it and do it now' is their slogan.

Procrastination is not part of their characteristics.

Choleric is very social, outgoing, open, friendly, personable, charming, inspiring, and charismatic but beneath the surface, they don't really like people. They appear to like people but in reality, they don't. They see people as tools which can be moved and used to accomplish their goals.

They are extroverts of highly selective nature. They approach many people for socialization, but they end up by selecting and moving with only those who meet their criteria, who can be moved into getting their goals done. They are highly social and inspirational, but they have little need for friendship.

Though they don't really like people, yet many people like them very well. This is because they are very inspirational, charismatic and charming; therefore, they use it to draw many people after them.

Choleric is task oriented. They relate to tasks and systems than to people. Precisely, they are tasked friendlier than people. And because they are task oriented, they are able to complete every task they set out to accomplish regardless of the cost or consequences.

They are tough minded and strong willed personalities; hence, they are not easily discouraged. When they make up their minds, they hardly change it.

They possess great leadership qualities and can do spirit or attitude. And because of that, they are able to exhibit good minds for envisioning new projects. They are also able to make intuitive decisions and carry out Considerable responsibilities: but they are shallow; they don't analyze details.

Choleric have a hard time admitting their mistakes; hence, they hardly apologize or say sorry. When they are **wrong, they hardly accept it.** They always think they are right. And because of that, they normally walk over the rights and feelings others.

Choleric have a great deal of control over the lives and behaviors of others, but they themselves, they tolerate almost no control over their lives and behaviors. In other words, they like controlling people, but they don't want anyone to control them.

Hence, they easily become angry if they are controlled, or someone interferes with their independence or in their affairs.

When they are undertaking tasks, they want total control over it; therefore, they tolerate very little or no interference from other people.

Choleric is self-centered. They are very confident in their abilities; and because of that, they normally feel the need of others do not matter.

They make decisions based on facts rather than emotions therefore; they seldom listen to advice to anyone else. They always want to have total control over themselves and anyone around them.

Choleric is of the opinion and belief that they know what is best for those around them, and acceptable behavior for them. They also believe that no one else can carry out a task as well as them; and because of that, they always want to take on leadership roles.

Because they relate to task than to people, they normally over work themselves; hence, they are highly susceptible to burn out.

Choleric do not move by feelings, emotions, conditions, situations and states of anyone. Theirs is the only way that is correct and matters to them. They are uncomplimentary. They hardly or freely give. In other words, they are headstrong.

When they are carrying out tacks to accomplish goals they normally undertake any behavior, be it ruthless, intimidation, or whatever necessary to get the work done.

They easily become very critical of anyone under their control, especially if tasks are not done to meet their standards.

Choleric **is** hot tempered. They easily externalize their anger and use it to lash out at anyone who try to control them or interferes in their affairs. They are bossy boots; but do not want anyone to bossy them; therefore, they externalizes anger to drive out anyone who try to bossy them.

They normally embark on behaviors like intimidation, yelling and the like to maintain control of others.

When Choleric is in authority, they appear to be uncaring, abusive and ruthless, yet they can be magnanimous and good leaders. The only flaw is, when they are in authority they normally fail to take care of the people they lead. They also look down on those who have less strength of will.

They normally become cruel to those who resist or reject their control.

Choleric is capable of solving problems and dealing with wrong and evil doers; hence, they always want to be leaders. And because they always want to be leaders; they prefer choosing and joining organizations and the association that will allow them to lead or head them. They like deciding for others. They also require recognition for accomplishment or whatever service they render.

They possess the will power to carry tasks to completion; but they are people users. They use people to get their way. When they are frustrated, they easily become angry.

Choleric are **bold**, judgmental, aggressive, unforgiving and hot tempered. They harbor anger a lot. They are also prone to violent and terrorizing.

Nevertheless, even though Choleric is unforgiving, yet they tend to be magnanimous especially when they are in authority; forgiving completely their opponents or antagonists.

Because do it and do it now is the slogan of choleric, they quickly move into action without thinking deeply about it first. Theirs is, the end justifies the means.

With the exception of anger, choleric seldom express emotions like compassion, love, tenderness, empathy, warmth, laughter, sorrow, and the likes. They see them as unnecessary, useless, and time wasting.

Choleric shows a great deal of love and affection, but they place conditions on the love they give and receive. They give and receive love and affection according to their terms.

They refuse to believe that people really love them unless the love is given in the way they believe it should be given; hence, they reject people and the love they show if they do not meet their terms or provide it according to their standard.

They have a hard time admitting or accepting deep, tender feelings like tears, hurt feeling, sorrow and views of others. They consider those feelings as sentimental trivia that are not called for.

They normally associate or develop deep relationships with people who are weak willed to get their own way, then after getting what they want, resent them for being weak.

However, in summary, Choleric is optimistic, open, friendly, confident, outgoing, tough- minded, task-oriented, upbeat type of personals, inspirational, charismatic, charming, strong will, bossy, impatient, hot tempered, inflexible, decisive, uncomplimentary, unsympathetic, intolerance, organizers, goal stimulators, self -willed, strong leadership abilities possessors, extroverts, selective, people users, capable of making intuitive decisions, capable of taking on responsibilities, leaders, hard-working, arrogant, aggressive, bold, proud, motivators, unapology renders, controversial, augmentative, not easily discouraged, possessors of tasks completion will power, anger harbors, unforgiving, unemotional, impetuous, dictators, courageous, self-sufficient, detail unconscious, fast-paced, production insisters, know- it all, practical solution seekers, independent, possessive of friends and mates, highly expressive, low responsive, challengers, serious, tasks and systems oriented, bored by trivia, compulsive change seekers, manipulators, disliking of tears, laughter sorrow and empathy, demanders, uncompassionate, practical solution seekers, production insisters, must correct wrong and can do attitude possessors, dynamic and active.

However, some of the choleric is: Apostle Paul, Dr. Kwame Nkrumah and Jerry John Lawrence.

SANQUINE

Sanguine are the cheerful, handshaking, touching, physically hold on to the listener, greeting and the most outgoing types of persons. They are very social. Among all the characters, they are easier to be around socially. They like greetings very well.

They believed that life is an exciting and fun filled experience that should be lived to the fullest. Hence, they enjoy socializing, shopping, going to places and being with people.

They live as though they have neither past nor future. They don't worry about the past or the future. They live in the present. And because of that, they seldom learn from their past mistakes.

Sanguine are prone to exaggerate. They like exaggeration, very well. They always exaggerate things. And because of that, they hardly recognize their failures, but rather, they exaggerate to make themselves appear to be more successful than they truly are. They even exaggerate their emotions and feelings. They scare a lot.

Sanguine are relationship oriented. They are human friendly than tasks and systems. And because they are relationship oriented; they suffer anxiety if they are forced to be away from people for a long period of time.

They are very talkative; and because of that, they always dominate conversations.

Sanguine are extroverts of highly intense. They enjoy free interactions and the company of others very well. They hate being alone. They like the company of others than being alone. And because they like being with people than being alone, they always seek out social contacts.

They are the life of the party. They bring life and energy into a room by their very presence. Their cheerfulness and humor brighten everyone's life. They have a very good sense of humor; hence, they are able to make fun, entertain and laugh at amusing things with a loud voice very well.

Sanguine are very fast-paced, active and restless, therefore, inactivity causes them stressful. A tired sanguine is a happy person. When they are stressed, normally, it is a change of environment that makes them recharge.

They are very Good speakers, communicators, storytellers, and entertainers; hence, they perform well on stage. They also excel in communication-oriented tasks. But they normally appear to be unserious.

Sanguine are warm, friendly, personable, fun, and upbeat type of persons. They freely interact with all types of people. They normally consider the good and the bright side of every thing and every one rather than the odds.

Sanguine are compassionates, generous, givers and loving. They relate to the feelings of others very well. And because of that, they normally do things for others almost to the point of servitude.

However, even though, Sanguine are compassionate and caring, yet they can be rude and uncaring. They also tend not to be faithful and loyal friends. This is because they don't want to be burdened down with commitments; they just want to have fun.

Sanguine are volunteers. They normally volunteer for tasks, especially difficult ones and try as much as possible to complete it as long as their ego is fed. But on the other hand, they don't normally accomplish what they volunteer for. They just volunteer for recognition and attention.

Because Sanguine likes fun, they normally ignore tasks and responsibilities in order to go to places to have fun and to be with people.

Sanguine like attention very much. They always want to be the center of attention, and because of that; they normally take on any behavior necessary for gaining attention.

They are also afraid of rejection; therefore, they normally adopt the behaviors of any crowd in which they find themselves in order to prevent rejection.

They have a short attention span; hence, they easily move attention from one person to another.

They are distracted and interrupters. They don't listen well, yet they frequently interrupt others.

Sanguine are quick tempered. They easily explode into anger, but forget it in few minutes. They don't normally hold grudges; neither do they release the past nor live in it.

They are optimistic; hence, they easily put aside or let the past, such as mistakes, failure, etc go and move on in life.

Nevertheless, even though, sanguine are optimistic, yet they easily lose confidence.

Sanguine are very forgetful. They easily forget things. They also like answering for others. They easily apologize.

They are relatively weak-willed: and because of that, they easily succumb to temptation. They hardly deny themselves. They decide by feelings and emotions. They are also controlled by circumstances.

Sanguine are naive and shallow; hence, they easily get taken in. They are easily impressed and overwhelmed; hence, they easily believe everyone. They hardly grow; in the sense that, they normally behave like children regardless of their age.

They are epicure-very interested in food.

Due to their fun loving nature, they normally fall into excess and hedonism; believing that fun is the only important thing in the world. They can truly love life than no one else.

Among all the temperaments Sanguine are the friendliest, approachable, undisciplined, unorganized, shallow and impulsive. They suddenly act without thinking about what might happen afterwards.

Sanguine enter into happiness when they are made the center of attention, accepted rather than rejected, has plenty of social interaction, employed in a situation that provides plenty of human contact, has plenty of activity, praised and honored for their achievements, paid complimented for their work, received plenty physical attention such as hugs and the like.

They thrive on compliment: hence they always want to be praised, recognized and honored for accomplishment.

Because Sanguine are people oriented, they have little understanding of tasks and systems. They get bored easily. Therefore, they always seek stimulation.

They like people genuinely. They are sincere at heart.

Sanguine express and require a large amount of love and affection. And because of that, they always want to establish and maintain deep personal relationships with many people. They require a great deal of physical expressions of love and affection such as hand holding, hugging, physical stroking and the like.

They respond to love, affection, acceptance and attention very well. They suffer anxiety if they are not regularly appreciated or told they are loved and needed.

They are very good at making deep relationships feel loved.

Sanguine are very positive with regard to establishing and maintaining relationships. If they are rejected by deeper relationships; they try as hard as possible to restore it back:

but if it does not work, they easily forget it and move on with the hope of getting another one.

They are very uninhibited when it comes to showing love and affection. They have a strong fear of rejection; therefore, they normally go against their own will by doing or telling people what they want to hear in order to prevent rejection.

They are highly emotional; hence, they usually act on the emotion of the moment without thinking about the end results of their words and actions.

They are people pleasers. Therefore, they normally develop behaviors and moralities of others in order to meet their needs for love and affection.

Among all the temperaments, sanguine are the most lovable and easy to get to know.

They value friendship, love, and close interaction, even more than physical possession. And because of that, they always need active and caring relationship where words and acts of love and caring emotions such as romantic walks, touching, holding of hands, appreciation and the like are on a regular basis.

They are quick to open up emotionally and respond to others willing to do same. Therefore, insufficient human interaction at an intimate level normally causes them devastation and all sorts of trouble.

Sanguine suffer or plagues with the feeling of jealousy when the love and attention they feel belong exclusively to them are given to others. They always need to hear, see, and feel loved and affection such as touch, acceptance, approval and the like on a regular basis.

Sanguine are fickle. They easily change their mind. They are also unstable and double standard. They swing like a pendulum from independent mode to dependent and vice versa. This means that, at times, they allow others to have control and to make decisions for them; but at times they also don't allow anyone to control and to make decisions for them.

When they are in the dependent mode; whereby they allow themselves to be control of others, during this time, they normally become self-indulgent, incompetence, irresponsibility and dependence. They sit back and entrust tasks which should be done by themselves to others to do it.

Then, when they feel worthless, they swing to independent mode.

When they are in the independent mode, they allow no one to control them. They become in total control.

During this time, they tend to be demanding, capable, dependable, aggressive, controlling, responsible, effective, and willing to assume nearly any responsibility or job and to perform it with a high degree of excellence.

They normally refuse any tasks, assistance; but eventually, when they draw near to burn out, and the task is too much, they feel used and this causes them to swing back into dependent mode.

This unstableness of dependent-independent and vice versa, of sanguine, does not normally make them able leaders.

They are the least in the world, especially the males when it comes to leadership. They are less than two percent in the world.

Whilst Sanguine is in authority or in control, they also want others to be in control. This attitude also is one of the reasons why they swing like a pendulum.

Sanguine normally take on a large amount of responsibility or volunteer for services in order to receive recognition but they don't normally perform what they have promised.

They take on responsibility and make a decision very well at some point; and because of that, they normally need a terrific amount of support, praise and commendation. If things go wrong or they feel insufficient appreciation for any service they have performed, they sink into a mire of self pity, drowning in a sea of resentment just because they felt used.

However, in summary, sanguine are very outgoing, friendly, warm, enthusiastic, expressive, emotional, demonstrative, approachable, inspirational, sincere at heart, optimistic, relationship oriented, talkative, impulsive, undisciplined, quick tempered, exaggerators, solicitors, charming, gracious, emotionally open, easily to get to know, fickle and forgetful, egotistical, good on stage, appealing personalities, story tellers, life of the party, distracters, volunteers, new activities thinkers, trivia dwellers, naive, always children, blusters, complainers, unorganized, fast confidence losers, restless energy possessors, cheerful, curious bubblers, physically holds on to listeners, elaborators, obligation forgetters, adaptable, changeable, good sense of humor possessors, interrupters, easily friend makers, haters of being alone, demanders of love and affection, story repeaters, active, prideful, seductive, highly expressive, highly responsive

Responsibility ignores, adventurers, materialistic, worldly, scattered, credit seekers, weak willed, conversation dominators, Preventers of dull moments, spontaneous activities lovers, and popularity seekers.

However, one of the sanguine is Apostle Peter.

MELANCHOLY

Melancholies are highly introverts. They are private and serious persons who always need quiet time to think, dream and regenerate. They have powerful thinking engines; hence, they are always thinking.

As their thinking process spins downwards or upwards, so do their mood, self-esteem and outlook on life.

Melancholies are very moody. Mood swings follow their thinking process. If they are thinking positive thoughts, their mood swings upward as well as if they are thinking negative thoughts, their mood swings downwards.

They possess strong, sensitive emotional nature. Feelings dominate their being. And because of that, they easily become moody, gloomy, depressed and offended.

As introverts or antisocial by nature, they don't approach many people for socialization; neither do they allow or give room for much socialization.

They always want to be alone rather than to socialize.

They are very selective when it comes to socialization. They are easily hurt, ashamed or embarrassed; and because of that, they hardly approach people for fear of any action that could be lead to embarrassment.

Melancholies are tasks oriented. They relate to tasks and systems than to people. In other words, they are tasked friendlier than people.

They approach life as a step by step task to undertake with an end result always in mind.

They are slow-paced and careful. They work at a steady slow pace and lose momentum as the day progresses.

They are self-motivated, self-disciplined and meticulous. They are very interested in details. They possess high intellectual thinking abilities; hence, they are able to think things out and see the potential pitfalls. They are also able to visualize things in their minds.

Melancholies are perfectionists. They are very interested in excellence, quality and beauty; and because of that, they depressed over an imperfection. And this depressed over imperfection, normally results in being critical of themselves and others if tasks are done shoddily

Melancholies are very sensitive, **vengeful, and unforgiving.** They are easily offended. **When they are offended or hurt, it pains them very well, especially when they recall it, and this normally causes them to be**

unforgiving. When they are offended in surface relationships or friendship, they normally remote or seek out revenge.

They don't easily forget or let go past mistakes, failures, hurts, insults, or offense. They relive negative experiences from the past. They brood on the past; dissecting it with theories.

Because they are easily hurt, offended and embarrassed, they normally weigh words and actions of others; hence, they are able to determine others minds, motives, etc. through their words, signs and moods.

Melancholies appear to be calm and quiet on the surface, but they are often angry and resentful. They are very dark personalities; therefore, they hardly reveal or share their secrets or issues with anyone. They are calm, but do not tolerate nonsense. They harbor anger a lot. They are easily angry, bitter and detest or abhorred. They are the doubting Thomas's who always need to prove. They are very doubtful, critics, curious, controversial, argumentative, and judgmental but very analytical.

When they are offended, the more they think about it, the more bitter and angry, they become; and this makes them unforgiving. They normally become extremely brilliant and inventive.

Melancholies are not easily convinced or persuaded; neither do they easily give up. They are rational, idealistic and uncompromising. They are moderate in expression, but able to express or articulate the unarticulated without fear.

They are strong minded. When they make up their minds, it is very hard to change it.

They don't respond to or move by promise of rewards or threats of punishments. They tend to take a more realistic viewpoint.

Melancholies **are very afraid of the unknown and failure.** They are pessimistic; **and because of that, they hesitate to start project. They normally choose difficult work in life. They are not satisfied with one accomplishment. They always think they can do more and better. They are not easily discouraged. When they start a task they always want to complete it.**

They normally know their limitations; therefore, they rarely take on more than they can do. **They have a deep need for approval**

Melancholies normally set high standards for themselves and even those around them. They also develop hard habits. These standards and habits are sometime hard to meet and to break.

They are very creative and analytical, but are prone to depression.

They are persecution complex. They always think that people are trying to harm them, and because of this mentality, they hardly believe or trust anyone.

Melancholies are highly independent minded and strong willed personalities. Due to their independent nature, they hardly submit to authority.

They express very little control over the lives and behaviors of others, and do not tolerate control over their lives and behaviors.

In other words, they don't normally allow anyone to control them for any reason; neither do they like controlling others.

They always demand order, truth, reliability and dependability from selves and others. They are intellectually oriented and detail prone; therefore, they are interested in facts, research, information, questions and the like.

Due to their intellectual or thinking capabilities, they normally follow and show respect for individuals and leaders whom they know to be intellectually superior.

Melancholies possess a very strong sad inner nature; and because of that, they easily feel sad. When they are sad, it normally last for a long period of time. Due to Sadness, they easily cry or explode into tears.

They are highly self-willed, self-centered and suspicious. Among all the temperaments, they are the most self-willed and self centered.

Nevertheless, even though they are sell-willed and self-centered, yet they have low self-image as well as suicidal tendencies.

They have a great fear of being wrong or making mistake; hence, they are very careful in their dealings or activities. When they are confronted for making mistakes, criticized or make to look foolish they quickly respond with anger.

Melancholies are legalistic, rigid, inflexible and uncompromising. Their extremely sensitive nature causes them to be easily insulted or offended. They are very suspicious; hence, they easily jump to unfounded conclusion. They suffer guilt when they offend others. They normally examine themselves to a very high degree; and this normally makes them energetic and inactive.

Melancholies have a very critical and challenging mind and great understanding of tasks and systems; therefore, they are able to see the pitfalls and the end results of a project undertaken.

They possess good leadership abilities. Hence, they easily make good decisions without delay. But if they are faced with making decisions about things or carrying out tasks they know little about, they tend to procrastinate it. After the procrastination, if they are forced or pressured to continue it, they easily become angry, upset and rebellious. They don't like those in opposition.

Melancholies adhere to the rules very well; hence, they hardly break rules.

They make considerable decisions and demonstrate good leadership qualities when they are operating in areas where they are well informed. They also demonstrate good leadership qualities and perform excellent tasks when they are operating in their own pace which is always slow and cautious.

Due to their intellectual and analytical abilities, they are able to see the end of a project before moving forward

However, although, melancholies are independent minded persons who do not allow anyone to control them, yet they normally put on masks to appear calm and in complete control to cover up any self doubt and perceived inadequacies. They are false humility demonstrators.

Melancholies are genius prone. None of the temperaments is capable of producing genius as the melancholies. Wherever an outstanding wisdom, knowledge and profound genius are seen, a melancholy is likely operating behind the scene. They are very curious. They always want to know; hence, they are very interested in research. They have very good memory for details; therefore they are very good at details. They are very creative and inventive. They are also very economical.

Melancholies rarely show or want physical expressions of love and affection. They regard physical touch as a part of foreplay; leading to sex otherwise it is considered nonsense.

They have very few deep personal relationships. And these few deep personal relations normally include spouse, children and possibly one or two good friends.

They possess very deep, tender feelings, but they seldom show or communicate how they truly feel. They struggle to express their deep, tender feelings.

If they show too much physical love and affection, they feel crowed as if their space is being invaded.

They express love and affection by performing tasks, being responsible and dependable.

Melancholies are very loyal, faithful and honest people, especially to their families and friends. When they make a promise, they keep it. They are true to their words.

They are self-sacrificing for both deep relationships and mankind as a whole. Due to their sensitive nature, they are able to empathize and identify with the feelings of others. And this normally causes them to commit themselves very deeply for others. They whole heartedly feel, commit and do things for all, irrespective of either any difference.

Melancholies hardly trust anyone; therefore, they hardly enter into deep relationships. And because they don't easily trust, when they enter into a deeper relationship, they regard it as very precious. And because deep relationships are very precious to them, when they lose the deep relationship they become devastated.

They express a great deal of faithfulness and loyalty to friends and even co-workers, but they normally demand same in return. Therefore, failure to do so or provide them the same honesty, faithfulness and loyalty, causes them to be angry which easily result in remote.

Melancholies are highly distrustful. They hardly trust anyone; hence, they always want others to prove themselves trustworthy before entering into deep relationship with them. When they are in deep friendship or personal relationship, on the surface, they appear cold and guarded, but in truth, they are tender hearted and caring.

Their demeanor and posture makes them appear eccentric; and because of that, many people shy away from them.

Due to their demeanor, very few people normally draw closer to them for friendship, but those who do so find themselves with fiercely loyal and faithful friends. But if they are hurt, injured, or offended in this friendship, they normally become angry and withdraw back or may seek revenge.

However, in summary, a melancholy is an introvert, a loner, great thinker, genius prone, artistic, creative, theoretical, vengeful, emotional, inflexible, philosophical, thoughtful, analytical, purposeful, conscientious, idealistic, self-willed, self-centered, poetic, self-sacrificing, economical, ideal mate seeker, careful, perfectionist, detail conscious, unforgiving, musical faithful, devoted, loyal, honest, antagonistic, thorough, suspicious, persistent, strong-willed, neat and tidy, orderly, organized, schedule oriented, moody, gloomy, prone to depression, introspective, intense, observer, investigator, insightful, detached, inventive, nihilistic, rebellious, guilt feeler, ,rigid, high standard setter, past reliever, rejecter,

Alienated, pessimistic, independent minded, sensitive, distrustful, cold, guarded, self-motivated, self-disciplined, disgustful, persecution complex, hypochondria, quilt feeler, false humility demonstrator, skeptical of compliments, attention causing avoider, shy, compassionate, and empathize, low expressive and low responsive.

However, some of the melancholies are: Moses and Solomon.

PLEGMATIC

Phlegmatic is calm, easy going, and steady as you go sorts of persons. They slowly and quietly proceed or go through life doing as little as possible without expending or using much energy. And because they expend little energy in life, they hardly and seldom put their gifts, talents and ideas into action since it requires much energy and effort to do so.

They appear introverted, yet they are able to socialize when the need arises. They are both task and relationship oriented.

They relate well to tasks and systems as well as to people.

Phlegmatic have great capacity for work that requires precision and accuracy. They are very tough minded. When they made up their minds; it is hard to change it.

They are able to identify injustice, wrong doings and things that need to be changed, yet they hardly and seldom initiate or take action against it. Instead, they try to inspire others to do something about the injustice and the wrong doings, but they don't personally get themselves involved.

They are very difficult to motivate. They make changes only when their minds command them to do so. Until their minds command them, they don't make changes, regardless what anyone says.

Phlegmatic is slow paced; therefore, they prefer working at a slow, steady pace and lose momentum as the day progresses.

They take a few chances. They also break few rules; hence, they lead safe but boring lives. They tend to be observers of life rather than doers. They are spectators. They like and enjoy watching people very well. They are teasers. They like to tease very well.

They are not easily upset or angry; and because of that, they are able to function in an unfriendly and hostile social environment quite well, nothing ruffles their feathers. They get tired easily. When they are tired, normally, it is only sleep that makes them regenerate. They like sleeping very well.

Phlegmatic express moderate amount of control over the lives and behaviors of others and allow a moderate amount of control over their lives and behaviors. In other words, they don't control people much; neither do they want others to control them much.

They take an easy approach to life. They don't over exert themselves. They work best if there is little pressure and risk.

They are able to perform boring and tedious work to higher degree. They are better off working undisturbed by others. They rarely volunteer for tasks.

Phlegmatic is capable of making decisions and taking on responsibilities, but they always prefer to share responsibilities and decisions with co-workers rather than doing it alone. They are team work referrers. They always expect others to work as hard as they do and to carry their part of the load.

When phlegmatic is to take action against popular opinion, they rather try to motivate others to take the action. This is because they lack the energy to take any real action themselves.

Phlegmatic are witty, sarcastic and humorous; hence, they use a dry, witty and sarcastic sense of humor as a defense mechanism to prevent others from motivating or controlling them.

Among all the temperaments Phlegmatic is the most stable and stubborn when it comes to making changes. They are changing resistors. They resist change very well.

They stubbornly refuse to move or change when they are asked to carry more than what they believe to be their fair share. They adamantly refuse to take on responsibilities or make decisions that are not theirs.

Phlegmatic is sanctimonious. A self righteous phlegmatic whose mind is already made up, is an impossible to move individual regardless of facts. They are very difficult to motivate. They always use verbal defenses, like witty, humorous and sarcastic against anyone who tries to control them. They are not easily angry or upset.

And because they are not easily angry; wit, humor and sarcasm are their weapons. They are able to make people, especially those who try to control them look amazing, uncomfortable and unpleasant. They have a good sense of humor; therefore, they are able to make fun and laugh at amusing things very well. They also laugh and make fun of others very well.

Phlegmatic is very practical, conservative, peace-loving and a good peace maker or arbitrators. While others or the other temperaments border on or call for violence, they border on peace. Peace at any price is their motto. Because Peace at any price is their motto, they are natural negotiators and diplomats.

They are sympathetic, kind, indecisive, anxious, selfish, shy, quiet, calm, compromising, inoffensive, peaceful, agreeable and very fearful personalities. They are prone to procrastination and laziness.

They don't like much social interaction; hence, they like remaining indoors. However, though they don't like much social contacts, yet they like making many friends.

Phlegmatic expresses and wants only a moderate amount of love and affection. They don't normally express or show their feelings. They hide their personal feelings behind a dry, witty and sarcastic sense of humor.

They are observers; hence, they don't involve themselves much in life, nor indeed relationship; neither do they exert, supply or expend much energy.

Due to their low energy supply, they don't normally involve themselves much in deep relationships. And because they don't involve themselves much in deep relationships, they normally use verbal defenses such as humor and sarcastic to protect their low energy supply with regard to or when it comes to physical and sexual involvement. They also use humor and sarcastic to avoid becoming too involved in relationships.

They use their dry sense of humor to hold their deep relationship at a safe distance where they will not use up their energy. They have little feelings for the people whom they involved with in deep relationships.

Phlegmatic are emotionally well-rounded; hence, they are able to tolerate people who show them a little love and affections as well as people who show them a great deal of love and affection. They are able to tolerate hostile and unaffectionate people very well.

They don't move by nor suffer and plaque with emotional outbursts, exaggerated feelings, anger, bitterness or unforgiving. They are very cool and complacent, and this cool and complacent attitude of them, normally hurt most of their lovers.

Phlegmatic is unemotional, inexpressive, non-self-sacrificing, well-balanced, easygoing, non-demanding, calm and realistic in demands for love and affection. They don't demand much for love and affection.

However, in summary, phlegmatic is a low-key personality, easy going, calm, cool, collected, patient, well balanced, quiet, witty, sympathetic, kind, shy, , fearful, worried, indecisive, forgetful, unenthusiastic, selfish, compromiser, reticent, self-righteous, peaceful, agreeable, inoffensive, viewer, change resistor, sarcastic, teaser, judgmental, relaxed and terrific friend, unaware of reality and problems, moderate in expression, gentle, lazy, careless, easy to get along with, discourager, conflicts avoider, all-purpose persons, stubborn, non-demanding, mediator, peace-maker, receptive, preservationist, Complacent, emotions hider, pleasant, enjoyable, good listener, dry sense of humor possessor, good under pressure, problem mediator, self motivation lacker, emotionally guarded, and well-rounded, sanctimonious, slow-paced, steady, administrative ability possessor, uninvolved, dampens enthusiasm, responsibility avoider, inexpressive, procrastinator, moderate expressive, moderate responsive and conservative.

However, Some of the phlegmatic is: Calvin Coolidge the thirtieth president of the United States of America, and professor John Evans Ata Mills the third president of the fourth republic of Ghana.

SUPINE

Supine is slow-paced and diligent. They are introverts in appearance, yet they desire much social contacts. Their demeanor and body language makes them look as if they don't need socialization; but the truth is they need it very much.

The issue is they don't have the ability to initiate or approach people for socialization. They find it difficult to approach people. And because of that, they always want to be invited or approached by others. They are very loyal, kindhearted and faithful.

They work at a steady slow paced and lose momentum as the day progresses.

They are relationship oriented and because they are relationship oriented, they suffer great anxiety if they are forced to be away from people often, or forced to be alone for a long period of time. They are easily devastated if they are excluded from social activities.

They have strong feelings of social contact but they are not able to express themselves. They are very sensitive; hence, they are easily hurt, insulted or offended.

When they are hurt, insulted or offended, they easily become angry; but instead of showing or voicing it out, they normally internalize or keep the anger within them, allowing them to be hurt by it. This anger is termed as hurt feelings.

Supine possesses high intellectual capacities. They are thinkers, but not as real or deep as the melancholy.

They are highly responsive. They are highly responsive to both threats of punishment and the promise of reward. If there is the promise of reward or a threat of punishment, they quickly change their actions in order to receive the reward or to avoid the punishment.

They are highly responsive to emotional rewards such as recognition, approval and acceptance. They are also highly responsive to emotional punishment such as guilt, rejection and loss of recognition.

They have a strong fear of rejection.

Supine are not aggressive. They become embarrassed when they are paid a compliment. They always want people to be real. They draw closer to people within a reason; but they find it difficult to express their needs. They have little ability to express their needs; hence, they always want others to know their needs by reading their minds. Failure to do so normally causes them offended.

Supine is moody. When they are moody, normally, it is only a change of environment that changes their mood.

They find it difficult to speak their mind.

They also find it difficult to say no. And because of that, they take more than they can do. They are service oriented, but they highly require recognition and appreciation for whatever service they render. Failure to do so causes them angry.

They are paranoid-always with suspicion and believe that people are trying to harm them especially in an unreasonable manner. They harbor anger very well.

They are easily upset. They always want to be organized.

They have low self esteem, and because of that, they constantly search the environment for messages to confirm that indeed they are not valuable persons.

They have a view of the world; and this view makes them consider others to be superior to them; hence, they employ themselves in positions that permit them to be servants to others. They dutifully work to please people who they see as better than themselves.

Supine requires a high amount of love, affection and approval and are capable of expressing high amounts either, but they do not initiate love, they are only responding. They express love by serving or performing tasks. They are non-assertive in a deep relationship.

They have the capacity to serve deep relationships, but they always require recognition and appreciation for their services. If they are not recognized for their service, they feel used; and this causes them to be angry.

They experience extreme loneliness and feelings of being unwanted; hence, they are always searching for messages to confirm that indeed they are not loved or needed.

Because Supine fails to communicate their needs for love, affection, attention, approval, etc., their needs normally go unmet.

Supine is faithful and loyal friends, especially if they are treated properly or appreciated. They appear reserved and cool, yet they are truly in need of a lot of close personal affection, love and attention.

If supine actually feels safe in a close personal relationship they respond and return expressions of caring. They become intensely loyal, producing absolute complete faithfulness. None of the temperaments is more prone to this kind of intense loyalty as the supine.

Supine is very emotional; therefore, they easily cry. They always require honesty in close relationships. They also require constant appreciation and reassurance that they are loved and needed.

They are easily offended and insulted. They appear cold and withdrawn, especially when they are offended; but in reality, they are not: they simply do that as a defense against the fear of rejection. They also do that to manipulate others to take care of them.

They have the ability to respond to love and to open up emotionally when they feel emotionally safe. If they are treated properly; they are capable of absolute and total commitment to deep personal relationships. They have an intense need and a very high capacity to serve associates and deep relationships.

Supine expresses little control over the lives and behaviors of others, but allow others to take control over their lives and behaviors.

They easily feel inadequate; therefore, they normally consider themselves incapable of making good decisions on their own; and because of that, they incline to seek out others advice when they are making decisions.

They normally seek out counsel from many people; then, when they receive different opinions, they become confused.

Supine hardly disagrees with anyone for being lazy, incompetent or morally weak. They also hardly blame or criticize anyone. They easily believe very one.

They are excellent team players, but they get lost in scapegoating. They don't want to be blamed. This attitude of fear of scapegoating, makes them to be betrayers, in the sense that, when there is an issue, they quickly exempt themselves, pretending as if they know nothing about it.

Because Supine always wants to serve and to please their associates and bosses, they find it difficult to say no to an issue or a command even if it is against their wish. This attitude of unable to say no is also due to their lack of ability, courage, and fear of rejection. And this inability of saying no easily causes them to be angry for feeling used.

Supine does not possess good leadership qualities; hence, they are not able to become good leaders. They are dependent. They depend on others to make decisions; hence, they have a strong need for close personal friend who will share decisions and responsibilities with them. **They have a very weak willpower; and this causes them to feel powerless; hence, they are always at the mercy of others.** And because they are always at the mercy of others, they have a strong fear of being left alone.

They feel they live in environments that want them to be responsible for their lives, but they don't normally feel confident enough to actually do so. This feeling also makes them find themselves at the mercy of others. It also makes them have a strong fear of being left alone.

Supine are natural born victims. They possess a very gentle spirit. They are typically slow to fight back; and because of that, they tend to internalize their anger and hurt, actually believing that they deserve the treatment they receive. And because they are not able to fight back, when they are young they are often tormented and abused by other children.

Supine is very dependable. They have abilities to enforce policies set by others and to serve those they follow. They are caretakers with absolute loyalty.

They are weak-willed; therefore, they are easily manipulated by guilt. They also use quilt to manipulate others.

Supine becomes extremely anxious when they are forced to make a decision and take on responsibilities independently. They easily become angry if they are not consulted about a decision that others make which involve them; yet they are hesitant to make the final decision; they only want their input considered.

They don't want to be blamed. They always want to please their associates and bosses. And this attitude normally makes them incompetent leaders.

However, in summary, supine is diligent, dependable, loyal, gentle, slow paced, very sensitive, kindhearted, rule keeper, unaggressive, loving, devil's advocate, faithful, excellent team player, introvert, responsive, caretaker, dedicated, possessive, manipulative, emotional, easily upset, moody, believer of everyone, shy, pleaser, rejection fearer, easily hurt, skeptical, complex, paranoid, scapegoating fairer, serviceable, thinker,

Inexpressive, inadequate feeler, victim, anger harbourer, slow to fight back, powerless feeler, unable to express themselves, constant reassurance demander, low expressive, high responsiveness, and weak-willed.

However, one of the supine is Mother Theresa.

Note, as at least two of the primary colors-white, red, blue, yellow, green, and black, are mixed together to form different colors such as violet, indigo, ash, etc., so do at least any two of the temperaments blend to produce a different character or temperament.

So therefore, not everyone is purely one type or hundred percent of any of the basic temperaments, which are choleric, sanguine, melancholy, phlegmatic and supine.

Some are blend or mixture of at least two of them. And this mixture is designated as: phlegmatic- sanguine, sanguine -melancholic, choleric- phlegmatic, supine- phlegmatic, melancholic- choleric, etc.

But since you now know the characteristics of the melancholy, supine, sanguine, choleric and phlegmatic, you can easily identify yourself as a choleric-phlegmatic, melancholic-sanguine, etc.

Now, any of the temperament appears to have its strength and weakness. And the weakness seems to be bad even though it is not because every human being was created by God for a specific task on this earth; so therefore, both the strength and the weakness were infused into every one as tools for the accomplishment of such tasks.

So, the weakness is not bad as appear, just that, it must be controlled and used to serve the purposes for which they were created rather than to offend others.

Christians, we are the light of the world, we have been bought with the precious blood of Jesus Christ for good works. Therefore let us be filled with the Spirit of God and walk with him in order to be able to control and use our inborn nature to fulfill its purposes to the glory of God.

BESIDE THE TEMPERATMENTS

However, beside the various temperaments, there are certain characters also. These kinds of characters or temperaments, differ from nation to nation, tribe to bribe and family to family. They are typically characterized or associated with nations, bribes and families. These temperaments are different from the basic ones.

These temperaments came into being through culture, tradition and norms. So therefore, due to cultural tradition and norms, citizens of every country is associated or characterized with a certain character which is different from the character of citizens of any other country in the world.

The same way, apart from the general character of every country, every tribe and family are also associated or characterized with a certain character which is different from any other tribe and family even within the same country.

Therefore, since every country, bribe and family has its own general character, act like Paul, study them, and act accordingly for the sake of peace and for your own betterment. It is written, "For though I be free from all men, yet have I made myself servant unto all, that I might gain the more. And unto the Jews I became as a Jew, that I might gain the Jews; To them that are under the law, as under the law, that I might gain them that are under the law; to them that are without the law, as without the law, (being not without law to God, but under the law to Christ,) that I might gain them that are without law. To the weak became I as weak, that I might gain the weak; I am made all things to all men, that I might by all means save some". (1 Corinthians 9:19-23).

Note: due to position, marriage, or help, many people normally wear masks to cover their inborn nature until they get what they want before exposing their real nature. Therefore, be familiar with the various temperaments to be able to identify everyone's character as well as those who put on the mask.

MESSAGE TO MEN CONCERNING WOMEN

However, beside the various basic temperaments and the general character traits that are associated or characterized with every country, bribe and family, which is common among all human beings, both men and women have peculiar separate character traits. This separate character traits of men and women were due to the separate tasks assigned to them by God to accomplish on this earth, especially the one spelled out in Genesis 2:18 which says, "And the LORD GOD said, it is not good that the man should be alone; I will make him a help meet for him".

Because of this assignment, women were made a little bit weaker to men, both physically and mentally for the sake of order. And because women are a little bit weaker to men, both physically and mentally, was the reason why the devil by-passed the man-Adam and went to Eve the woman.

So apart from the various temperaments and the general character traits of every country, tribe and family, men have their own character traits and women also have theirs: but only the character of the women is considered here. Even, out of the character of women, only a fraction of it is considered here.

This fraction of the character of women was exhibited by Eve the first woman, in the Garden of Eden even before sin entered the world. It is written, "Now the serpent was more subtle than any beast of the field which the LORD God had made. And he said unto the woman, yea, hath God said, ye shall not eat of every tree of the garden? And the woman said unto the serpent, we may eat of the fruit of the trees of the garden.

But of the fruit of the tree which is in the midst of the garden, God hath said, ye shall not eat of it, neither shall ye torch it, lest ye die. And the serpent said unto the woman, ye shall not surely die:

For God doth know that in the day ye eat thereof, then your eyes shall be opened, and ye shall be as gods, knowing good and evil. And when the woman saw that the tree was good for food, and that it was pleasant to the eyes, and a tree to be desired to make one wise, she took of the fruit thereof, and did eat". (Genesis 3:1-6)

Now, according to the above scripture, Eve was moved to eat the fruit of the forbidden tree by the sugar quoted words of the serpent, and the goodness and attractiveness of the fruit. And this attitude of Eve had been common among women since then till today.

Men, with exception of sexual emotions, women easily believe, act and move of what they see and what they hear, especially sweet and attractive things and because of that, they are easily deceived.

Because they easily believe, act and move of what they see and what they hear, especially sweet and attractive things in all angles, absence of sweet and attractive things in marital homes makes them unhappy and uncomfortable, and this normally results in all kinds of problems.

This character trait of women, makes them appear to be troublesome and problematic; but that was how they were made; therefore, men, especially husbands, do not see them as troublesome, but rather, know them by nature and live with them accordingly for your own betterment; for it is written, "Likewise, ye husbands, dwell with them according to knowledge, giving honor unto your wife, as unto the weaker vessel, and as being heirs together of the grace of life; that your prayers be not hindered." (1 Peter 3:7)

CHAPTER TWO

PEACE MEDICINE

Peace is the most important commodity in the world. It brings growth and development in life, society, tribe, community, family and a nation as a whole. But where there is offense, anger, unapology, unforgiving and lack of love, peace cannot exist.

For this reason, this book has been written to draw all human beings, especially Christians, to the consequences of offense, anger, lack of apology, forgiving and love in order to refrain from them to pay way for peace to reign in our societies, families, nations, and the world as a whole.

OFFENCE

Offense is an act of upsetting someone. It is the source of anger which when uncontrolled, causes a lot of atrocities. Many people have lost their lives, many nations have been destroyed, many marriages have been broken, and many people have lost great opportunities just because of offense.

Offense is dangerous, therefore, try as much as possible to avoid it.

People become offended through discrimination, insult, cheating, injustice, unfairness, disdain and the like. All of these are sources of offense.

Where there is offense, there is no unity and peace; and where there is no unity and peace, there is no development.

For this reason, try as much as possible to avoid all kinds of actions and words capable of generating anger.

Jesus Christ, the owner and the Saviour of the world himself, paid taxes to avoid offense. It is written,

"And when they were come to Capernaum, they that received tribute money came to Peter, and said, doth not your master pay tribute? He said, yes. And when he was come into the house, Jesus prevented him, saying, what thinkest thou, Simon? of whom do the kings of the earth take custom or tribute? of their own children, or of strangers. Peter said unto him, of strangers. Jesus said unto him, Then are the children free.

Notwithstanding, lest we should offend them, go thou to the sea, and cast an hook, take up the fish that first cometh up; and when thou hast opened his mouth, thou shalt find a piece of money; that takes and give unto them for me and thee". (Math. 17:24-27)

If Jesus Christ, the Lord of lords and king of kings paid tax to avoid offense, then, why do we intentionally offend one another?

As it is written in Philippians 2:5 that "Let this mind be in you, which was also in Christ Jesus," let us therefore emulate the example of Jesus Christ, and it will be well with us.

Note, it doesn't matter your position, stature, financial status, educational background, etc., offense can cause a lot of damage in your life. One abusive word or offensive action can set a nation ablaze, can set families, couples and friends apart, can cause a lost of position, etc.

Many heads of state have been overthrown, many kings have been dethroned, many heads of institutions and organizations have been sacked, and many marriages, families and friends have been split just because of offense.

For this reason, try as much as possible to avoid offending by checking your words, actions and deeds for the sake of peace and your own betterment. It is written, "Who is the man who desires life, and loves many days, that he may see good? Keep your tongue from evil, and your lips from speaking deceit.

Depart from evil and do good: seek peace and pursue it". (Psalm 34:12-14. 1Peter 3:10)) It is also written, "He who guards his mouth preserves his life, but he who opens wide his lips shall have destruction". (Proverbs 13:3, 21:23)

Therefore, for the sake of peace and unity which bring development in life, society, family, etc. and your own well-being, avoid all kinds of abusive words and offensive deeds, and it will be well with you.

ANGER

Anger is a strong feeling of being insulted, treated unfairly and the like that makes someone to hurt, destroy, damage, kill, etc.

Note, Anger is one of the aspects of human nature; therefore, we cannot do away with it. For this reason, the Bible says in Ephesians 4:26 that, "Be ye angry and sin not; let not the sun go down upon your wrath." This means that, since anger is part of our nature, we may be annoyed, but we should control ourselves without acting abnormally in anger; neither should we harbor anger in our hearts against one another.

Where there is anger, there is hatred and all kinds of atrocities. Peace and unity which bring development in life, society, family, etc., are completely absent in the environment of anger.

Note, anger itself is not evil. It was created for a specific purpose. Jesus Christ, therefore demonstrated to us one of the purposes for which anger was created by using anger to override the hypocrisy of the Pharisees to heal on the Sabbath day. It is written, "And he entered again into the synagogue; and there was a man there which had a withered hand. And they watched him, whether he would heal him on the 'Sabbath day; that they might accuse him. And he saith unto the man, which had the withered hand, stand forth.

And he saith unto them, Is it lawful to do good on the Sabbath days, or to do evil? To save life, or to kill? But they held their peace.

And when he had looked round about on them with anger, being grieved for the hardness of their hearts, he saith unto the man, stretch forth thine hand. And he stretched it out: and his hand was restored whole as the other". (Mark 3:1-5)

So therefore, anger was not created for evil deeds, but rather, to serve as a defensive and protective apparatus against nuisance and injustice as well as a force to enforce the right thing to be done.

But as far as anger is not being used for the purpose for which it was created, there is nothing good in it, but downfall, loss of opportunities, broken homes, failure in life, imprisonment, etc.

However, since we are human beings, someone may offend you, but never react abnormally and turn to be a fool at the end. For it is written, "Be not hasty in thy spirit to be angry; for anger resteth in the bosom of fools. It is also written; "He that is soon angry dealt foolishly." ((Ecclesiastes 7:8, Proverbs 14:17a)

Be patient and self-controlled in all circumstances, and you will turn to be victorious and successful in life. (Proverbs 14:29a, 16:32)

Anger causes a person to lose a lot in life. It is a very terrible thing which everybody must try as much as possible to control. Many people had been in prison, some are still in there, many people have lost their lives, many people have lost great opportunities in their lives, many marriages have been broken, and many nations have been destroyed just because of anger.

Moses, who was described by God as the meekest person in his era, a man through whom God delivered the Israelites out of the land of Egypt, never entered the promise land because of anger.

When God delivered the Israelites out of the land of Egypt through Moses, they rose up against him since there was no water in the wilderness to quench their thirst. For this reason, Moses went into the presence of God, and God said unto him, "Take the rod, and gather thou the assembly together, and speak ye unto the rock before their eyes, and it shall give forth his water, and thou shalt bring forth to them water out of the rock: so thou shall give the congregation and their beasts drink.

However, Moses therefore took the rod and gathered the congregation together before the rock as he was commanded by God, but due to anger as a result of pressure from the children of Israel, having gathered the congregation together before the rock, he said unto them, "Hear now, ye rebels: must we fetch you water out of this rock?

Then, having said that, he lifted up his hand and smote the rock with the rod instead of pointing it to the rock and speaking to it. (Number 20:2-12)

And because of that, God said unto him, "Because ye sanctified me not in the eyes of the children of Israel, therefore ye shall not bring this congregation into the land which I have given them. Hence, due to anger Moses never entered the promise land.

So therefore, since anger is not being used for the purpose for which it was created, but rather being used more for offensive and hurtful purposes, it is expedient for us as human beings to avoid or control it for the sake of peace, unity, development and for our own good.

APOLOGY

Apology is something that a person say or write to an offended person to show him or her that he or she is sorry for offending him or her.

Where there is no apology; there is no peace and unity. Apology quenches anger. It is written, "A soft answer turns away wrath". (Proverbs 15:1)

But unfortunately, many people find it difficult to render an apology with a rationale that such act renders them inferior. And because of that, many nations have been destroyed, many people have lost their positions, many people have lost their lives.

Note, it doesn't matter your financial status, position, popularity, educational background, etc., lack of apology will cost you dearly: therefore, learn to render an apology.

Since we are human beings, we are therefore subjected to human error, and because of that, you will by all means offend someone. When such an incident occurs, put everything aside, accept your fault and apologize as the Bible admonishes us to do for our own good. It is written, "Therefore, if thou bring thy gift to the altar, and there rememberest that thy brother hath ought against thee: leave there thy gift before the altar, and go thy way; first be reconciled to thy brother, and then come and offer thy gift". (Matthew 5:23:24.)

An apology will not render you inferior; neither will it take anything out of your life. It will rather enable you to gain more respect. Therefore, husbands, heads of states, kings, parliamentarians, ministers of states, reverend ministers, leaders of institutions and organizations, directors and employers, put your headships, position and everything aside, accept your faults and apologize for the sake of peace, unity, development and your own god.

Jacob offended Esau his elder brother for snatching his blessing, the blessing of the first born son, and because of that, Esau wanted to kill him; it is written, "And Esau hated Jacob because of the blessing and said in his heart, the days of mourning for my father are at hand, then will I slay my brother Jacob". (Genesis 27:41)

However, Jacob, having been aware of this, ran to Padan Aram-Syria to sojourn there. Then on his return back home after a number of years in Syria precisely two decades, with a great possession and a great number of servants, did not consider his wealth, but put them aside and went to render a sincere apology to Esau his brother. And Esau forgave him and accepted him as his brother again. (Genesis 27:1-46, 28: 1-10, 32: 3-6, 33:16)

For this reason, do not hesitate to render apology; for apology takes away the anger.

Note, the Bible says in Proverbs that, "He who covered his sins shall not prosper, but he who confesses and forsakes them will have mercy. The same way, unapology gives room for bitterness and hatred, but apology enforces anger to give way for peace to reign.

Therefore, friends, couples, leaders, etc., let us therefore accept our faults and mistakes and apologize; for it is the only way peace and unity which bring development in life, society, family, tribe and a nation as a whole, can reign.

FORGIVING

Forgiving is an act of ceasing the feeling of angry with an offender. Where there is forgiveness; peace, unity, health and development are common; but its scarcity, generates all kinds of atrocities which normally result in imprisonment, sickness, death, broken homes, etc.

So therefore, unforgiving is one of the cardinal causes of a person's downfall, suffering, failure, disgrace, and difficulties in life as well as a hindrance to most of our prayers.

It is written, "For if ye forgive men their trespasses, your heavenly father will also forgive you: But if ye forgive not men their trespasses, neither will your father forgive your trespasses". (Matthew. 6:14-15.)

This means that, the prayer of a person with anger in his or her heart against someone is unacceptable to God. God doesn't answer those who harbor anger in their hearts against their offenders: So therefore, for the sake of peace, unity and your own good forgive.

Forgiving creates an avenue for love, peace, unity, development, health and respect.

Nelson Mandela, the first president of South Africa was imprisoned for twenty seven years for calling for independence and the abolition of apathy, yet when he became the president, he did not hold it against the colonial masters who imprisoned him. He forgave them; and this made him the most popular and respected man in his era and even beyond.

For this reason, forgive always no matter the degree of the offense.

Peter said unto Jesus, "Lord, how oft shall my brother sin against me, and I forgive him? Till seven times? Jesus said unto him, I say not unto thee, until seven times: but, until seventy times seven." (Matthew. 18:21-22)

This simply means that we should always forgive without holding grudge against our offenders.

Unforgiving can hinder you from entering heaven. So therefore, do not behave like the wicked servant, whom his lord (master) delivered to tormentors to be tormented for refusing to forgive his fellow servant's trespasses immediately after his master had forgiven him his, lest you be cast into hell. It is written, "Then his lord, after that he had called him, said unto him, O thou wicked servant, I forgave thee all that because thou desiredst me: shouldest not thou also have had compassion on thy fellowservant, even as I had pity on thee?

And his lord was wroth, and delivered him to the tormentors.

So likewise shall my heavenly father do also unto you, if ye from your hearts forgive not every one his brother their trespasses." (Matthew 18: 35)

Note, forgiving is a medicine. It is both preventive and curative medicines in all dimensions physically, mentally and spiritually; therefore, do not harbor anger for the sake of your own good.

Since we are human beings and subject to human errors, people may offend you; but whether it be tensions or intentional, conscious or unconscious, do not hold grudge nor harbor anger; but rather, let it be known to the offender if possible and forgive no matter the degree of the offense and whatever the response may be; for the sake of peace, unity, development, and your own well-being.

LOVE

It is written, "Behold, how good and how pleasant it is for brethren to dwell together in unity". (Psalm 137)

Unity brings peace and development in life, society, family and a nation as a whole: but unity cannot exist without love. **Love** is the source and the belt of unity. Therefore, where there is love, there is unity, and where there is unity, there is peace and development.

Love is defined by Oxford advanced learner's dictionary as a strong feeling of deep affection for something or somebody.

Nevertheless, love has been divided into different categories by some people; but the truth is, love is love. It is unconditional. Therefore, it is written, "Love your neighbor as yourself; for if ye love them which love you what reward have ye."(Matthew, 5:46, John 13:32)

Since love is unconditional, its Absent is the main causes of partiality, discrimination, selfishness, uncompassionate, callous, cheating, etc., in societies, institutions, organizations and nations which normally generates all kinds of problems such as sabotage, hatred, arm robbery, fraud, etc. Therefore, leaders of societies, institutions, organizations and nations, try as much as possible to embark on love for the sake of peace, unity and development.

Love binds people together as one man with one soul, one mind and one spirit, irrespective their educational, financial, racial, tribal, religious, cultural and socio-political backgrounds and differences; and this makes impossibility possible. It is written, "Behold, the people are one and there is nothing that they cannot do". (Genesis 11:1-3)

Love is the means by which a nation, an institution or organization is developed. It is the source of development. No nation can be developed without love. Lack of love is the main reason why many nations are not developed.

Note, discrimination, selective-justice, partiality and the like which are as a result of lack of love, cause all kinds of pains and bitterness, and because of that, people may come together or appear to be one in body but completely different in spirit and in mind; and this negatively affects growth, progress and development.

Therefore, for the sake of peace, unity and development and your own good, love all irrespective of any differences as Jesus Christ, the greatest man ever lived admonishes us to do.

It is written, "Ye have heard that it hath been said, thou shalt love thy neighbor and hate thine enemy. But I say unto you, love your enemies."

Love is not selfish, discriminatory, nor self-seeking but rather, it does things for the interest and benefits of all and because of that, shoddiness, bribery and corruption, bitterness and all kinds of social vices which breech and cripple peace, unity and development are rare or uncommon in the environment of love; therefore, put on love.

Note, people cannot be one without love. And where there is no oneness or unity, there is no peace and development because 'every kingdom, nation, society or family divided against itself cannot stand', therefore, individuals, heads of states, Reverend ministers, leaders of institutions and organizations, for the sake of peace, unity, development and our own good; let's put on love, and it will be well with us.

About the Author

Daniel Nana Kwame Opare is a citizen of the family of God, the body of Christ. He is a philosopher, Bible scholar, an ardent and a prolific writer.

He is divinely ordained to reveal the mysteries in the word of God for revival and transformation of individuals, the church and the world as a whole. His books are highly written for spiritual, physical, mental and material transformations of lives.

Some of his books are: What every believer must know, Enlightenment and Success garden, and, The Secret of greatness.

www.ingramcontent.com/pod-product-compliance
Lightning Source LLC
Chambersburg PA
CBHW072111290426
44110CB00014B/1889